DORSET
MOODS

PETER THOMAS

HALSGROVE

First published in Great Britain in 2003

Title page photograph: Windsurfing near Portland.

British Library Cataloguing-in-Publication Data
A CIP record for this title is available from the British Library

ISBN 1 84114 315 4

HALSGROVE
Halsgrove House
Lower Moor Way
Tiverton, Devon EX16 6SS
T: 01884 243242
F: 01884 243325

sales@halsgrove.com
www.halsgrove.com

Printed and bound in Spain

DEDICATION
This book is dedicated to my friend, the late Richard Bridle,
who acted as navigator on our countless trips to Dorset
and came to love the county.

INTRODUCTION

The opportunity to undertake a photographic project on Dorset was to be an eye-opening experience. For many years my focus had been entirely centred on Devon and I had rarely visited Dorset. Over a period of three years I visited about 170 sites across Dorset, from dawn to dusk. The most spectacular aspect of the county is the coastline, with some of the finest coastal scenery you will see in Britain and now designated as a World Heritage Site. It is famous for its palaeontology (fossil hunting). However, the countryside is rich with numerous charming villages and small towns. The chalk-based earth gives an entirely different feel from Devon and landscapes tend to be more open.

A number of vantage points such as Golden Cap, Eggardon Hill, Maiden Castle and St Catherine's Chapel at Abbotsbury give stunning panoramic views across the county. At Studland there are fine views over the heathland to Poole. Possibly the most dramatic setting for any castle is at Corfe where from the hills you look towards the sea and over the distant countryside.

For those interested in building, architecture and history, the county has a proliferation of excellent examples of country cottages, manor houses, castles and other buildings. At Stanbridge is a fairy-tale thatched cottage, at Sherbourne the abbey and castle and at Iwerne Minster a group of interesting properties relating to the Arts & Crafts Movement. For enthusiasts of early churches there is a diminutive church, with a lovely rustic interior, at Winterborne Tomson, and the Norman church at Wareham with the effigy of Lawrence of Arabia in Arab costume. For elegance and history the Elizabethan Parnham House, near Beaminster, and also Athelhampton, are well worth visiting. Intriguing features in the landscape include a massive folly at Horton, near Cranborne, the Clavell Tower overlooking Kimmeridge Bay and at Cerne Abbas, the famous Giant.

Delightful gardens are found across the county. Minterne Magna with its wandering garden, bluebells and bridge is a delight in the spring, and for variety and colour there is Compton Acres at Bournemouth. At Pamphill, the estate village to Kingston Lacy, there is a fine oak avenue, part of a lovely woodland setting integrating some of the finest cottages in Dorset. The rivers of Dorset have traditionally operated mills and good examples are found at Maiden Newton, Hinton St Mary and a working mill, open to public, at Mangerton. The Dorset Steam Fair at Tarrant Hinton is one of the county's most colourful events.

A visit to the county should include, if possible, a trip to Portland as it has its own special atmosphere and the finest view you will see of Chesil Beach. For lovers of wide-open landscapes, the sea and coastal walking, the coastline of Dorset is stunning. From Handfast Point overlooking Poole Bay can be seen one of the county's famous coastal features – The Pinnacles, white chalk stacks standing proud out of the sea. At Durlston Country Park the full impact of the white chalk cliffs is seen towards Worth Matravers, St Aldhelm's Head and Chapman's Pool. The isolation of Kimmeridge has its own special atmosphere. A lovely horseshoe bay exists at Worbarrow but at Lulworth Cove you will see one of the most visited sites in Dorset and, adjacent to it, the most famous natural feature in the county, Durdle Door and Stair Hole, created by geological force.

Beyond Weymouth the famous Chesil Beach extends to Abbotsbury, providing nesting grounds for rare seabirds. At Charmouth the beach and surrounding cliffs have become a paradise for fossil hunters. With all this, and more, the county of Dorset has so much to offer and there is no doubt that it is not only rich in coastline but countryside, wildlife, architecture and history, with a wealth of fascinating places to visit.

Peter Thomas
May 2003

LOCATION MAP

Dawn across Marshwood Vale near Morcombelake.

Rich countryside in Marshwood Vale.

In the valley at Morcombelake the local farmer, Mr Fry, was producing stooks
in preparation for thatching. The delightful valley below Golden Cap
was facing the threat of a possible new bypass.

Harvest time near Abbotsbury, looking towards Lyme Bay.

On the steep coastal paths of Purbeck, wooden handrails assist the walker.

The Dorset chalk hills are nationally famous for their special art forms cut out of the hillsides down to the chalk level.
At Osmington can be seen the equestrian figure of George III.

Cerne Abbas is famous for its club-wielding, 180ft-high Giant cut through the turf of the local hillside.
His origins are unknown but it is thought he might date back to Roman times.
The Cerne Abbas Giant is one of England's most famous early historic images.

The atmospheric Eggardon Hill *(above and opposite)* is the site of
an ancient hill-fort and gives commanding views across the
Dorset countryside towards Golden Cap.

From Eggardon Hill the timeless beauty of the Dorset countryside stretches as far as the eye can see.

Opposite page:
Autumn colour at Symonsbury Hill, West Dorset.

Dramatic skies at Knoll near Abbotsbury.

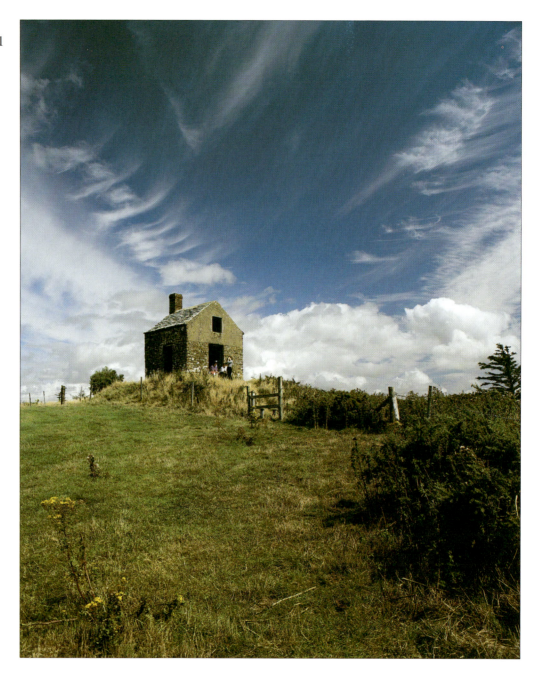

Broad, open landscapes are seen at Cann Common near Cranborne Chase.

The B3157 passes through fine countryside, shown at harvest time. The view is from the Knoll near Abbotsbury.

View from A35,
Littlebredy.

Middlebere Heath at Arne in Purbeck is typical of the important heathland that provides a habitat for the smooth snake and the sand lizard, two of the rarest reptiles in Britain. Dorset and its heathland are strongholds for both species.

Lush, rolling countryside can be seen at Pilsden Pen.

Taking the more rustic road B3159 from Dorchester to Weymouth you
will come to the village of Upwey. On this road stands an imposing
thatched stone barn with its walls supported by buttresses.

Opposite page:
From Bulbarrow Hill panoramic views look unfold
towards the Blackmore Vale.

Maiden Castle, near Dorchester, is the county's most impressive
Iron Age hill-fort. From its elevated ramparts there is an
uninterrupted view towards Dorchester.

Arne Woods in early spring, near Poole Harbour.

At Poole Quay stands the
fine Custom House with
two curving front staircases
and portico, at the junction
with Paradise Street.
It was rebuilt in 1813
after a fire destroyed the
original building.

In Market Street, Poole, a number of historic and characterful properties can be seen, leading the eye through to the mid-eighteenth-century Guildhall.

At Hinton Parva, on the B3078, stands one of the prettiest rustic cottages in Dorset. The thatched Lodge at Stanbridge, surrounded by early iron railings, features two domed, thatched porches, Gothic-style windows and an informal country garden.

This rustic thatched cottage at Stanbridge, Hinton Parva could be straight from the pages of a fairy-tale.

One of the most visited attractions in Bournemouth is Compton Acres, a series of themed gardens –
from Japanese and Roman to heather and cacti – created around a house built in 1914. The popular
Italian Garden has a classically harmonious and tranquil air with its fountains and water lilies.

The gardens of Compton Acres are superb and popular all year round.

To the north of Okeford Fitzpaine, off the A357, is the charming hamlet of Hammoon. The main attraction is the sixteenth-century Manor House, shown here in the autumn.

The sixteenth-century gabled porch of the Manor House of Hammoon is highlighted by the late-afternoon sun.
The property also incorporates seventeenth- and nineteenth-century additions. The adjacent church of St Paul
dates from the thirteenth century.

The town of Sherborne is dominated by stone buildings of various periods but the most impressive is Sherborne Abbey. Dating from the twelfth century its architecture is mainly of the fifteenth century. It is one of the most visited churches in the county. Nearby is the delightful complex of buildings known as St John's Almshouses.

Opposite page:
Milton Abbey, at Milton Abbas, is the remains of a fourteenth-century church but with nine-teenth-century additions. There are particularly fine interior monuments, especially the reclining figure of Caroline Damer. The arcading and floor tiles shown date from 1865.

The tiny church at Winterborne Tomson, near Bere Regis, originates from the twelfth century but with later additions. The altered interior dates from the early-eighteenth century and is one of the most charming in Dorset.

Forde Abbey, near Chard, is a substantial building dating back to the twelfth century, of which only part remains.
The building was altered in the seventeenth century and contains fine interiors with panelling,
paintings and decorative plasterwork. The 40 acres of gardens are well worth a visit.

At Charminster, near Dorchester, traditional building techniques are still much in evidence. These cottages are classic examples of banding work in flint and sandstone, used together with thatch.

Overlooking the famous Chesil Beach, in Fleet, stands the remains of the village's old church, attractively framed by a low wall and graceful pine trees. It was originally the vault of the Mohun family. The village itself, and new church, are known to many from the pages of the classic smuggling adventure tale *Moonfleet* (1898) by John Meade Falkner.

East of Portesham stands an impressive seventeenth-century house
built below the hills. Constructed from Portland stone, it has an
imposing stepped entrance guarded by two canine statues
and at the time of this visit two guardians of the real variety.

Parnham House, near
Beaminster, is set
in lush woodlands. The
elegant Elizabethan
building was landscaped
with gardens in the
early-twentieth century.
Parnham House
has been the home of
John Makepeace,
the furniture maker.

Horton Tower, near Cranborne, is a six-storey brick-built folly dating from the mid-eighteenth century. It was built to provide a lookout over the local hunt for the landowner, after he had retired from riding with hounds.

In the grounds of Abbey Farm at Cerne Abbas can be seen the remaining porch of the Abbot's Hall. The romantic structure still retains its magnificent two-storey oriel windows bearing carved coats of arms.

Minterne Magna House is situated in a fertile valley near Cerne Abbas and was built in the early-twentieth century, replacing a Victorian version. The property is better known for its extensive gardens.

Early spring at Minterne Magna Gardens.

Integrated into the small village of Wimborne St Giles, on the edge of
Cranborne Chase, is a village green, church and almshouses.
Built in 1624, the almshouses were constructed with ten single rooms and
bear a coat of arms on the front of the brick-built loggia.

Pamphill, near Wimborne Minster, is an unspoilt area extending over three commons. It is the estate village to Kingston Lacy and a delightful area. Dispersed amongst mature trees is a variety of brick-and-timber houses and cottages. There is also a superb avenue of oak trees.

The Oak Avenue at
Pamphill leads
magnificently to
the church.

A view of Chideock on the A35.

The impressive Kingston Lacy, near Wimborne, is one of Dorset's most important properties owned by the National Trust.
The seventeenth-century building resembles a French château, with fine interiors and extensive grounds.

Without doubt, the ruin of Corfe Castle is one of the most evocative in the country. Standing in the hillside gap that divides Purbeck from the rest of Dorset the setting is spectacular. From the castle interior views over Purbeck and the surrounding countryside are unparalleled. Construction of the castle started in the late-eleventh century and continued until the late-thirteenth century but was much altered in the sixteenth century.

The oldest postbox in the country, dating from the 1850s, can be found at
Holwell on the A3030 Sherborne to Sturminster Road.

At Rampisham is found one of the most picturesque post offices in the county.

The hilltop village of Ashmore, at Cranborne Chase, has as its central feature a large pond. Local geese take a stroll from their home there to graze on the lawn of the fine Georgian rectory.

Witchampton, lying off the B3078, is a village dominated by brick, although beside the church there are a number of timber-framed cottages. The short church tower features banding in flint and stone created in the mid-nineteenth century.

Evershot, in West Dorset, has an interesting variety of buildings and is
famous for the cottage where Hardy's Tess of the d'Urbervilles had breakfast.

Tess Cottage, adjacent to the church at Evershot.

Powerstock in West Dorset, a mix of seventeenth-, eighteenth- and nineteenth-century houses,
is situated around a group of small valleys.

In the Frome Valley stands the impressive remains of a three-storey fortified manor house called Woodsford Manor. Built in the fourteenth century, and already described as a ruin by the seventeenth century, only one side of the building now remains.

Milking time at Mapperton, near Beaminster.

The extensive buildings of the old mill, spanning the River Frome at Maiden Newton,
have now been converted to a private house.

Iwerne Minster, near Cranborne Chase, has an interesting mix of late-nineteenth century brick and timber-framed buildings that reflects the Arts & Crafts Movement.

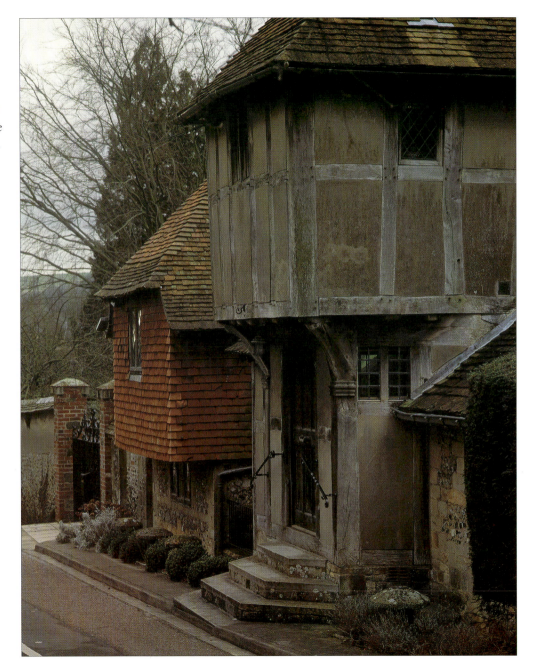

The village of Milton Abbas is a row of well-kept cottages with communal front lawns running down the main street. The village is known for the adjacent large abbey and eighteenth-century house built in Portland stone.

Christchurch Priory is the longest parish church in England, dating from the late 1100s to the mid-1600s. It has significant Norman features but the tower is fifteenth century. Christchurch Priory is one of the principal attractions in the area.

Cattistock, near Maiden Newton in West Dorset, is particularly noted for its church, one of the finest in Dorset. The tower can be seen from a considerable distance. The fifteenth-century building was rebuilt by Sir Gilbert Scott in 1857.

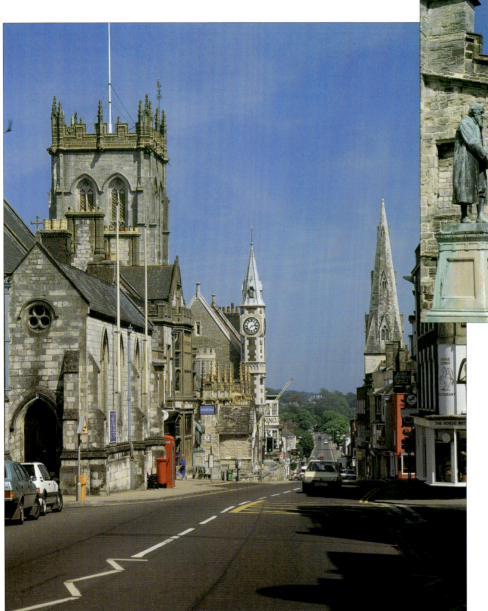

On the outside of St Peter's Church stands the statue of Dorset poet William Barnes, erected after his death in 1888.

Left:
The centre of Dorchester is dominated by a number of towers belonging to the churches of St Peter's, Holy Trinity, All Saints' and the clock tower of the old Corn Exchange.

The new Sherborne Castle was built by Sir Walter Raleigh in the 1590s.
The original building was later enlarged by adding corner turrets and in 1625 the new owners,
the Digbys, added further turrets, considerably enlarging the building. An elaborate stone gateway
was also constructed to create an impressive entrance. The castle, which was again extended
in the nineteenth century, contains numerous interesting interior features.

Mangerton Mill.

Each year at Tarrant Hinton the county's most colourful event is held. The Dorset Steam Fair draws thousands of people who come to admire the huge variety of steam-driven engines and vehicles. The event runs into the night, with a fairground operated by steam-traction engines.

Athelhampton, near Puddletown, is a fine late-fifteenth century house of
comfortable proportions, with alterations made up until 1920. This popular
attraction has formal gardens and a delightful laburnum grove.

Riverside walkway at
Christchurch.

Portland Museum is housed in a thatched stone cottage, dating from the mid-1700s, that has connections with one of Thomas Hardy's novels. Outside the entrance are examples of petrified wood extracted from the Purbeck Beds.

The church of St George Reforne on Portland is a prime example of the use of the island's famous stone. Built in the mid-1800s the large main body of the church is plain but it is enhanced by a decorative tower and was described by Pevsner as 'the most impressive eighteenth-century church in Dorset'. The headstones, also of Portland stone, are well worth viewing.

Portland stone, from the island of the same name, is internationally recognised for its quality and many highly important buildings locally and nationally have been built from it. Portland Quarry is one of several on the island.

Portland Quarry.

Standing on Portland Bill, the 135ft-high lighthouse, is one of the most
popular attractions. It was built in 1905.

On Portland, putting boats to sea is not quite so easy. Due to the extent of shallow cliffs along the coast it is necessary to use hoists to lift boats over the edge on to the sea.

No visit to Dorset would be complete without visiting Portland. It has a distinct character and numerous interesting aspects. The best views of Chesil Beach are from the heights of Portland.

The area around Portland offers excellent potential for water sports.

Looking towards Handfast Point, Swanage Bay.

Excellent opportunities exist in Swanage Bay for maritime activities and good views of the famous white chalk cliffs.

Near Peverill Point, Swanage, stands the Wellington Clock Tower removed from London in 1854 and re-erected in 1866. The structure no longer contains a clock.

Much of Dorset's
coastline is only accessible
to walkers. The area
overlooking Ringstead
Bay is owned by the
National Trust and offers
stunning coastal views,
and in the spring
a wealth of cliff flowers.

As with much of the British coastline, the shoreline at West Bay has been affected by winter storms and climate change. To protect the resort massive rocks have now been deposited on the beach to form a defensive barrier from the sea.

The most imposing feature of West Bay is the impressive weathered sandstone cliffs.

Detail of sandstone cliffs at West Bay. The Jurassic Coast of Dorset has been designated a World Heritage Site owing to its extraordinary geological features.

The sheltered horseshoe-shaped bay of Lulworth Cove, with its white chalk cliffs, is one of the most famous coastal attractions in Dorset.

The delightful Caundle Brook at Hinton St Mary provides an excellent habitat for
water lilies that are shortly about to flower.

Opposite page:
At Hinton St Mary one of the county's brooks was harnessed to operate New Cut Mill.
The brook and the mill provide an idyllic country scene at the rear of the village.

The village of Abbotsbury attracts hundreds of tourists annually.
Star attractions are the Swannery, church, abbey remains and the
Subtropical Gardens. The magnificent Tithe Barn, one of the
largest in England, has been converted into a museum.

The Subtropical Gardens at Abbotsbury, covering 20 acres, are among the county's
most visited attractions. Close to the sea, its displays of a wide range of flowers,
shrubs and trees from around the world is a delight.

Abbotsbury, as seen from the south-west.

One of the finest views you will find in Dorset is from St Catherine's Chapel above Abbotsbury.
On a clear day it is possible to look to Portland over the expanse of Chesil Beach.

Golden Cap, named after
the golden sandstone,
is the highest sea cliff in
Dorset at 618 feet.
Owned by the National
Trust, this superb natural
site should not be
missed by any visitor
to the county.

Golden Cap is shown with the small village of Seatown to the east.

Some of the best coastal walking in Dorset starts from
Durlston Country Park where the views are spectacular.
The prominent white chalk cliffs are a major feature.
This view is towards Swanage.

Right:
Durlston Country Park at Durlston Head leads to the
South West Coast Path and to Worth Matravers.
The spectacular coastline is owned by the National Trust.
A stone globe is a feature in Durlston Country Park.

Lighthouse at Durlston Head.

One of the most famous geological features in Dorset is seen at Handfast Point at The Foreland. A series of white chalk pinnacles, the result of natural erosion, stand isolated offshore.

Coastal views at Chapman's Pool near Worth Matravers.

The rounded bay of Chapman's Pool lies on a quiet part of the Dorset coastline just beyond Worth Matravers. The superb setting offers protection and seclusion for visiting yachts.

Charmouth, a short distance from Lyme Regis, takes its name from the River Char where it flows into the sea and is a favourite haunt for fossil hunters. Charmouth Heritage Coast Centre operates from the beach and is devoted to educating the public about Dorset's geology and natural history.

The popularity of Dorset's coastline for visitors can also create problems
due to erosion of the cliffs by visitors, a problem seen at Stair Hole.

Stair Hole, adjacent to Lulworth Cove, is one of the most well-known geological features in the county, the result of huge geological forces folding the earth's crust.

The village of Tyneham, situated below the Purbeck hills, has been deserted since 1943 when it was taken over as part of an army firing range. Because of the absence of human activity it has become a wildlife haven. The village leads to Worbarrow Bay where on this summer's day a nightingale could be heard singing in a scrub wood near the beach.

The cliffs and pinnacles from Ballard Down, Purbeck.

Dancing Ledge Quarries, situated near Langton Matravers, is one of a number of cliff-face quarries that were used to extract limestone, often using explosives to create access tunnels.

The view looking from White Nothe towards Bat's Head provides one of the reasons why Dorset's coastline has been designated a World Heritage Site. No one can fail to be impressed by this unique coastline.

Worbarrow Bay.

An unusual building stands in isolation at St Aldhelm's Head. This square
Norman chapel was at one time in the nineteenth century
used as a coastguards' store but later restored.

Studland, is renowned for its extensive areas of heathland, and in the eastern section there is an extraordinary feature called the Agglestone. Situated on a small hill a 500-ton piece of sandstone dominates the whole the area. It has been the subject of conjecture as to how it arrived there or whether it has always stood on this site. Rumours of meteorites and possibly the idea that it has been dropped by Satan are associated tales.

Right:
Detail of the Agglestone.

From Studland Beach the white cliffs of Handfast Point are seen.

The delightful town of Wareham is situated between the rivers Frome and Piddle and is
popular for its riverside pubs and boating.

The church of St Martin's at Wareham is a well-preserved Saxon building dating from 1030. The tower is a fifteenth-century addition. Inside is a life-size statue of Lawrence of Arabia (T.E. Lawrence) lying dressed in traditional Arab costume. He died in 1935, having spent the last years of his life at Cloud's Hill.

Wareham Quay.

A short distance down the River Frome from Wareham Quay is a delightful location which is the site of The Priory, a sixteenth- and seventeenth-century building, now converted to an hotel.

The coastline between Lulworth Cove and Bat's Head has some the of finest cliff scenery
in the county. The white chalk cliffs and geological features are stunning.

Opposite page:
Late afternoon at Swyre Head Beach.

The famous geological feature Durdle Door attracts thousands of visitors to the Jurassic Coast, now designated a World Heritage Site.

Durdle Door.

On the most easterly point of Purbeck, overlooking Studland Bay, are Old Harry Rocks, formed by natural erosion. The larger is Old Harry with the smaller Old Harry's Wife nearest the sea. Bournemouth is shown in the distance.

Old Harry Rocks.

Charmouth Beach, a fossil hunter's paradise, has a distinctly prehistoric atmosphere.

Osmington Mills, a short distance from Weymouth, is one of the first access places to the sea.
There are extensive views over Weymouth Bay.

Huge, rounded boulders are a feature of the shoreline at Osmington Mills.
This is the start of some of the region's most undisturbed coast.

Rock pools at Osmington Mills offer yet more to
explore on this fascinating coastline.

In the early spring the cliff-top flowers near Bat's Head burst into bloom.

Lyme Regis has acquired a national reputation as a centre for
palaeontologists (fossil hunters) and a number of shops
cater for an increasingly popular hobby.

The small seaside town of Lyme Regis stands at the border with Dorset and Devon and is a highly popular summertime resort offering an unspoilt location, a good beach, and safe swimming.

Fishing nets on the Cobb at Lyme Regis.

Lyme Regis offers good opportunities for boating, water-skiing and other water-based activities.
On the outside of the town are good coastal and country walks.

A number of elegant period seaside cottages overlook the sea at Lyme Regis.
A group known as Madeira Cottages is particularly noteworthy
on Marine Parade, dating from 1840.

The Cobb, the most famous feature of Lyme Regis, creates an artificial harbour protecting vessels from the sea. Originally built in the thirteenth century from wood piles and stone, it was replaced by a Portland stone structure in the 1820s. It famously featured in the film *The French Lieutenant's Woman*.

Lyme Regis, on the border with Devon and Dorset, is shown looking towards Golden Cap.
The recently designated Jurassic Coast extends from Exmouth in Devon to Portland.

The Esplanade at Weymouth, created in Georgian times, offers all the amenities of a traditional seaside resort –
whelks, jellied eels, ice-cream, donkeys, Punch & Judy and a safe place to swim.

Opposite page:
Weymouth Harbour is today a bustling tourist honeypot combining local fishing boats,
yachtsmen and quayside attractions.

Geraniums and the cast-iron clock erected for Queen Victoria's Golden Jubilee in 1887 are features of Weymouth's sea front.

Traditional Punch & Judy is still a firm favourite and attracts the crowds.
One of the leading exponents of this art, Guy Higgins, has
entertained thousands of people on Weymouth Beach.

Bournemouth, Dorset's largest and most visited seaside resort, was created in the early-nineteenth century from an area of heathland. Today the resort has a population of over 150 000. The beach and pier are always popular attractions.

Boat and spring flowers at Kimmeridge Bay.

Kimmeridge Bay, looking eastwards towards the Clavell Tower.

Opposite page:
The extensive, Kimmeridge Bay, is overlooked by a well-known landmark
on the eastern cliffs, the Clavell Tower. It was built as a folly in the 1820s.

On a quiet day at Kimmeridge, devoid of people, the silence was broken by the voices of singing nuns who were making their way down the cliff path!

Kimmeridge Bay, surrounded by shallow dark cliffs, has a very distinct feeling of
isolation and perhaps eeriness. Slightly isolated, with no beach, it has in
the past been referred to as 'the haunted bay'.

A mix of dark rock and sandstone gives Kimmeridge its own atmosphere.